THE
PLAGUE
COLUMN

THE
PLAGUE
COLUMN

by
Jaroslav
Seifert

translated
from the Czech
by
Ewald Osers

introduction
by
Sir Cecil Parrott
KCMG, OBE

photographs
by
Gilman Parsons

TERRA NOVA
EDITIONS
LONDON   BOSTON
1979

Edition © Terra Nova Editions Ltd
25, Upper Montagu Street London W1
English translation © Ewald Osers
Introduction © Sir Cecil Parrott

Printed and Bound in Great Britain by
W & J Mackay Ltd Chatham

ISBN 0–906490–00–6 (cased)
    0–906490–01–4 (limp)

This English version has been prepared in
accordance with Seifert's own definitive text of
1977, and incorporates many alterations from
previous texts circulated in samizdat form

I give the right to publish the translation of my volume "The Plague Column" to whichever firm is prepared to do so under the conditions customary in the USA.

Jaroslav Seifert

A régime which attempts to silence its country's greatest living poet sins against high heaven. In Vienna they may have thrown Mozart into a pauper's common grave, but at least they did not stop him from publishing his music. In Prague, at the age of 77, Jaroslav Seifert, today and for the last twenty years, indisputedly the greatest Czech poet of his age, has had to resort to *samizdat* to get his latest collection of poems published.

"The Plague Column" was first circulated in this form in Czechoslovakia a few years ago. In 1977 it was published abroad for the first time – in Germany and in the original Czech. Now, thanks to Mr. Osers' skill, patience and understanding, we can read it in a fine English translation.

The system of the "padlock" was frequently applied to writers in Russia in Tsarist times, as we can recall in the case of Pushkin, but it has become much more widely practised there under the Soviets. Indeed the treatment meeted out to Pasternak and Solzhenitsyn, to mention only those who are best known, is now applied to writers in other lands, who happen to have the misfortune to be held in the Soviet protectorate. It is these whom the Soviet régime has the least right to censor. What makes Seifert's case a crying injustice is that he is essentially a lyric poet and these poems which have had to be smuggled out are purely autobiographical and carry no political message. Indeed they become political only by the fact of their suppression.

But Seifert's work is banned not for what he writes, but on account of his "profile", which has long made him, if not an "unperson", at least a writer in semi-disgrace. He started life as a protégé of the Communists, a natural proletarian poet – a quality much appreciated by the Party in the twenties, and which the Communist idealist, Jiří Wolker, described by some as a "petty bourgeois dreamer", greatly envied. He had written of Seifert's first poems that they were created "out of working-class life, working-class blood and working-class fists". But to the dismay of his Communist patrons this young working-class song-bird began to change his tune and go his own way. Communism rarely forgives those who forsake its path, but what made Seifert's crime the more heinous was that he eventually joined the Social Democrat party, that party, from which in the twenties the Left Wing had seceded to become the Communist Party. The Communist Minister of Information, Václav Kopecký, wrote in 1963, that it would have been understandable if Seifert had joined the National Democrats or the Catholics on the far Right, but the Social Democrats – why, it was unforgivable. For one thing, it was not known that that party had ever had any poets!

Jaroslav Seifert belonged to that great generation of lyric poets, which included Halas, Nezval and Hora, all of whom were born at the same time at the very beginning of this century and attained manhood at the end of the First World War. Some of this generation were just old enough to be called up and some even put on uniform, but they only came in to witness the débacle and ensuing demoralisation.

Born in August 1901 in a poor family in Žižkov, a proletarian suburb of Prague, Seifert quickly won fame with a volume of verse about Prague called "City in Tears", in which he movingly described at first hand the misery of the oppressed classes and exulted in the coming revolution which would wipe away all their tears and transform the world into a heaven on earth. He was undoubtedly very much at home in this milieu, but, as he proved so elo-quently, he could also see beyond it. As a boy he used to spend his Saturdays sitting on the pavement outside the taverns in "our lousy Žižkov quarter", listening to the sentimental songs and ribald ditties coming from inside. He recalls this in "The Plague Column", where he writes:

"On the steps of the Olšany taverns
I used to listen at night
To the coffin-bearers and grave-diggers
Singing their rowdy songs,
But that was long ago,
The taverns fell silent
And the grave-diggers in the end
Buried each other."

He used to stay there until the evening, when his mother came and marched him off to church, perhaps to attend the May Festival of the Virgin, so that "after the smell and clamour of the taverns I found myself all at once in clouds of scent from the flowers and incense and was carried away by the charm of the baroque music". No wonder that he was afterwards reproached for using the imagery of the Bible in his verses. But this was held against Wolker and Neumann too, who have a firm place in the Communist pantheon. The teachings of Comenius die hard in Bohemia and Moravia.

After "City in Tears" Seifert was naturally expected to remain one of the Party faithful, but in 1923, after visits to France and Switzerland, where he fell under the spell of Rimbaud and Apollinaire, and indeed translated some of the latter's writings, he joined the group of "Poetists" in Prague, of whom Vítězslav Nezval was the guiding spirit. At the time the Party did not perhaps consider this to be a serious deviation, since Czech leftist poets continued to draw their poetical inspiration from Paris, while owing their political allegiance to Moscow. Moreover it was still Communism's boast that it was the creed of the *avant-*

garde. Had not Vančura written in his preface to Seifert's poems: "Outside Communism there can be nothing modern"?

In explaining Poetism Nezval had declared that the taste of his generation for metaphysical thought had been killed by the War. The old, conventional poetry of ideas was in their eyes nothing but a pack of lies. Beauty was henceforth to be sought through the senses and particularly the sub-conscious. But while disclaiming that they were surrealists or Freudians, the Poetists could hardly conceal the debt they owed to futurism, Apollinaire and Dada.

None the less for Seifert in particular it was an abrupt change from lamentations on the miseries of proletarian life and glorification of the heroism of working-class mothers to an uninhibited plunge into bourgeois hedonism, where "everything is happy and beautiful" from glamorous coquettes in jockey dress to the Eiffel Tower and Wagon Lit Sleeping and Dining Cars. An exotic collection of poems from this period appeared under the title "On the Waves of the T.S.F.", later republished as "The Wedding Journey".

Perhaps it was hoped that a visit to Moscow in 1925 might provide a corrective to the poet's wayward fancies. But the Russian comrades found that the book of poems which he published on his return, "The Nightingale Sings Badly", the title of which echoed Cocteau, barely concealed the author's disappointment with the Revolution. It seemed to them deplorable that he should have been fascinated by Moscow's old churches, abandoned "noble-men's nests" à la Turgenev and flea-markets, and that instead of being fired by the Revolution he was frightened of it and indeed appalled by its blood-shed. In his eyes Russia was "the graveyard of history".

The breach with the Party was bound to come sooner or later. It took place in 1929, when with six other distinguished leftist writers, including two of the most eminent of them, Hora and Neumann, he signed a manifesto criticising the Party leadership of Clement Gottwald. Subsequently all the signatories except Seifert and Hora confessed their errors and were forgiven. Of the two unrepentant sinners Hora left "Rudé právo" to join the Czech Socialist paper "České slovo" and Seifert gave up his editorship of Neumann's illustrated weekly to become a member of the Social Democratic Party. The Communists found it particularly hard to forgive Seifert, because rightly or wrongly they believed him to have incited the others to sign the offending manifesto.

In the volumes of verse which he subsequently published – "The Carrier Pigeon", "Apple from the Lap", "Hands of Venus" and "Goodbye Spring", which filled in the next eight years until 1937, Seifert settled down to the genre and form of poetry which he was to adopt for most of his life – pure lyric poems on scenes of everyday life and the thoughts they aroused in him, interspersed with memories of his boyhood, his mother and his home; often ballad-like in form and sometimes deceptively simple, tossed off with apparent lightness but always exquisite, pure and fresh, their moods varying from the playful and paradoxical to the mournful and nostalgic. There was something of Horace's love of rustic enjoyment, something too of Anacreon's devotion to the muses, love and wine. As time went on the poet became more elegiac – more and more conscious of the youth that was deserting him. *Tempus fugit!* And the precious hours which remain must be counted and stored.

If Seifert appeared to have ceased to be a committed poet, he did not let the great and tragic national events of his country pass unrecorded. In 1937 he published a moving series of ten poems called "Eight Days", in which he voiced the grief of the whole of the Czech people at the passing of their beloved president, Thomas Masaryk, from the day of his death to his burial at Lány. In the fateful years which followed from 1938–1945 he wrote many poems which appeared subsequently in collections under various names. In these he bade farewell to his youth and touched lightly but feelingly on the pain and bitterness of Munich. Among them is a calendar of simple eclogue-like poems dedicated to the months and a batch of twelve *pantoums* (Malayan quatrains) on love.

Under the German Protectorate, in common with other leading Czech poets, he celebrated the 120th anniversary of the birth of Božena Němcová in a set of poems called "Božena Němcová's Fan", in which he portrayed the great Czech writer as a symbol of her oppressed country and a source of consolation and faith in its culture. His two other main works in this period were "Clothed in Light" and "The Stone Bridge", in which he paid homage to the beauties of his native city. Some of these poems were re-issued in 1945 in a collection called "Earth-filled Helmet", which contained additional poems commemorating the May days of the liberation of Prague; "The Barricade of Chestnut Blossoms", "The Prague Rising", "The Morning Song of the Red Army" and "The Coming of President Beneš".

Seifert was often musing on the beauties of old Prague and the legends of Bohemia. He wrote fantasies on the Loretta, the look-out tower on the Petřín, the famous astronomical clock in the Old Town Square, the Belvedere and the Waldstein Garden. He conjured up visions of St. Wenceslas, Dalibor, the Řip Hill, from which Father Čech came down, Ctirad and Šárka, Oldřich and Božena. He dedicated a poem to the four wives of the Emperor Charles IV. Perhaps no other Czech poet wrote so feelingly of the beauties of Bohemia or its great history. He dedicated innumerable poems to leading contemporary poets but never forgot the great ones of the past like Vrchlický,

Neruda or Mácha. He had a special eye for art and artists: all his collections of poetry were illustrated by the leading artists of the day – Josef Čapek, Svolinský, Jiřincová, Wiesner, Zrzavý, Kremlička, Kotík, Trnka and Janeček. In 1949 he devoted a set of verses to Aleš's paintings called "The Painter Went Poor into the World", inspired by the widely loved spelling-book the artist had illustrated. He was much attracted by the primitive, rustic illustrations of the Czech countryside executed by Lada, who became famous as the illustrator of "The Good Soldier Švejk", and celebrated them in his verse.

From 1945 to 1949 Seifert was an editor of the Trade Union daily "Práce", which was not then exclusively Communist-oriented, as I can personally confirm. I often used to call on its foreign editor, who was a friend of the West. Little did I know then what a short distance separated me from the back-room where Seifert worked, but I had only just come to Prague and knew nothing about him. I came regularly into touch with his fellow-poets, Halas and Nezval, because they were members of the Communist Party and occupied senior posts in the Ministry of Information. I well remember the contrast between these two Moravians, Nezval, large, ungainly, ebullient and noisy, and Halas gentle, retiring and loveable. As I was to learn later, Seifert was closer to Halas.

In 1947 a Czech friend gave me a copy of Seifert's "The Apple Tree with the Cobweb Strings" and read me some of the poems in it, which were dedicated to Halas. I never forgot the beautiful poem, with which the collection opened:

> "Whoever says goodbye
> Waves a white handkerchief.
> Every day something is ended,
> Something beautiful is ended . . .

Dry your eyes
And smile through your tears.
Every day something starts again
Something beautiful starts again."

Twenty-six years later, after I had got to know Seifert, I asked him to sign my copy of the book so that I could place it beside the others he had generously given me.

In 1949 Halas died. He had had many difficulties with his minister, Kopecký, who objected to his links with prominent persons outside the Communist ranks and to his independent views. He was criticised after 1948 for failing to glorify the Communist take-over and for living in the past, although he had in fact done a lot for the movement after the War, but no doubt the "Victorious February" sickened him. Seifert wrote a poem mourning his passing, but only a year later the dead poet was the target for a vicious attack by the leading Party ideologist of that time, Ladislav Štoll, who wrote him off as "a corrupter of the youth". "How is it possible," he asked, "that his poetry is still acclaimed by some critics, even in the Communist press, as the peak of Czech poetry?" From then onwards Halas disappeared from the ranks of the elect.

After Seifert had published in 1950 his exquisite "Song of Viktorka", which was a further tribute to the genius of Božena Němcová, the Party hack, Ivan Skála, accused him of "sinking even deeper into his subjectivism and his apolitical attitude, refusing to recognise the eduational role of art and focussing his attention not on reality but on the glittering fragments he extracts from it . . ." "Seifert does not see the joy of our working man," he continued. "He does not see his heroism, his optimism, the marvellous new qualities germinating in our people, nor the grand and happy prospect for the morrow." After this outburst

Seifert was not allowed to publish any new poetry until 1954, when a collection of poems about his working-class mother, "Maminka", was permitted.

Two years later the Second Congress of the Czechoslovak Writers' Union was held, under the direct impact of the XXth Congress of the Communist Party of the Soviet Union, at which Khrushchev had made his secret speech against Stalin. The Czech writers adopted a stand which led to their first important clash with the Party leadership. The trend of their discussions was that almost all Czechoslovak literature had been ruined by dogmatism and that the writers had been forced to act against their conscience. Seifert's speech at the Congress, and some private remarks he made outside it, were regarded by the Party as an attack on the new Socialist literature and the leadership. It caused considerable consternation at the top.

After that Seifert could expect to have no more new poetry published. In the years 1956–1959 his collected past works were issued in five volumes. In the sixties he wrote: "For a long time I have written no verses. Years ago I put down my pen and they put in my hand a thermometer ... How many people who were once close to me are already dead and I myself am already old. I don't write so easily as I did. And a greater feeling of artistic responsibility holds back my pen as it moves across the paper. I am not so carefree when I write as I once was."

Seifert was ill and still is. At the medical centre where he was being treated a young nurse asked his name. When he told her, she looked at him and in a rather severe tone asked him to repeat it. "And do you like poetry?" she went on. When he said he did and asked her in some surprise why she wanted to know, she replied, "Because of the kind of name you have."

To commemorate the Soviet invasion of 1968, Seifert

reissued his requiem to Masaryk in a special edition with Josef Čapek's original illustrations and his "Songs of Prague" with vignettes by Zrzavý. In 1969 he was elected President of the Union of Czechoslovak Writers, the last free president until the Soviet *Gleichschaltung* took place under Gustáv Husák.

He still lives on, a sick man, but not completely forgotten by the powers that be. In 1974 some of his works were included in an anthology called "A Thousand Years of Czech Poetry". It would have been difficult to exclude him from it, although he was given rather short measure in the collection. In the brief unenthusiastic note on him one reads the words: "He acted in sharp conflict with his proletarian origin and youth and mainly with the best aspects of his work both in 1929 and at the end of the sixties (when he lent his considerable authority as a poet to the anti-Party and anti-Social policy of the Right Wing leadership of the Union)."

Perhaps on reading the story of his life the reader may think that Seifert, as a dissident, was in fact a political poet and not the lyricist, which I have shown him to be. But the Party ideologists had reproached him all his life for not being political enough and what he tried to do at the Union of Czechoslovak Writers and as its President was to preserve literature from becoming a mere tool of political dogma.

A foreigner can sense that there is something classic about Seifert's verse. It has been said that at its purest it reaches the heights of Czech melodic speech and that his pedigree descends from Sládek, Neruda, Hálek and Toman. Czecks believe him to be one of the most Czech of Czech poets. His limpid style is very hard to translate. The critic Hanuš Jelínek, who translated Czech poetry into French, wrote: "On regrette que ce genre de poèmes échappe à toute possibilité de traduction Ce n'est plus de poétisme, c'est de la poésie authentique, pure et profonde." I should like to pay my homage to Mr. Ewald Osers for achieving the impossible and translating Seifert's work with such fidelity and understanding.

Cecil Parrott

25 November 1978

At one of his readings a long time ago
Jiří Mahen whipped out a copy of
Lidové Noviny:
he rolled it into a funnel and,
as if through a loud-hailer, exclaimed:
"Long live poetry!
                    Long live youth!"
That time that youth was still our own.

In those passion-flamed years our lives
were burning up more quickly.
Jiří Wolker was the first to die.
We spoke at his coffin.
It was January and a hard frost.

I hurried away from the grave as if
the sexton's coffin-slings were snaking
behind me in the snow.
I ran to the railway station
so that, as soon as possible, I might
put my head on your body's blossoms.

I read my poetry to Josef Hora
when his coffin stood before us
in the Hall of Fame.
I read it over his grave
humbly and quietly.
From the Fortress Wall near the cemetery
there is a splendid view of Prague
and to the north lies Říp Hill
as if tipped out from a child's hand.
It belongs to every one of us
but Josef Hora has a special claim.

My love that time was for
the Maytime meadows near Libuně
and for those modest hills all round:
Kozákov, Tábor, Bradlec, Kumburk
and the gentle uplands.
All day we'd wander aimlessly around
and when no-one was about
my lips would pounce on yours
and hungrily seek your burning tongue.
And tall before us, like a burnt-out lyre,
towered the ruin of Trosky.

When Halas was dying
I wrote a few quiet lines for him
about our youth.
They weren't particularly good
but they were the last he read.
He smiled as people smile when they know
they'll soon be dying. To this day
his wistful smile
follows my verses.

I wrote whatever I could:
at window tables in cafés,
on ink-stained desks at the post office,
with the telegraph ticking.
But best I liked writing at home.
You'd sit by the standard lamp
and I could hear your needle piercing
the stretched canvas.
Sometimes you were jealous of my poems.
They'd drift about with God knows whom
and God knows where
and you were so close, so very close,
no more than two, three paces.

Have you ever watched a guitarist?
The way he softly puts his palm
across the strings
and they all fall silent.
I have crossed the threshold
of that inexorable moment
and in my mouth there is a bitter taste
as if I'd bitten through a stalk of wormwood
that I could not break.

THE SCREAM OF THE SPECTRES

In vain do we reach for wind-blown cobwebs
and for barbed wire.
In vain do we dig in our heels
so we shouldn't be dragged quite so brutally
into the darkness that is blacker
than the blackest night
and lacks its crown of stars.

And each day we meet someone
who gratuitously asks us
without opening his mouth:
When? How? And what comes after?

Just one more moment to dance and prance
and breathe the perfumed air,
even with a noose round your neck!

In the dentist's waiting room
I saw in a torn illustrated paper
a rose-red terracotta statuette
I'd seen one like it once
in a case at the Louvre.

They'd found it in the marble tomb
of a young girl
who died long before Christ was born.
The baked-clay figurine knows all about death.
It could tell a tale. It stays silent
and smiles.

When the girl died
she must have heard the scream of the Empusa
who used to haunt the ones about to die
and guarded our graves.
She had one metal leg
and one of donkey dung
and screamed as the shades of the dead scream
on the banks of the Acheron.

Of course, the ancient spectres are now dead –
but new ones are being born.

Hello, operator, you didn't catch that?
Em – pu – sa.
I will spell it for you:
 E – as in erotic
M – as in mistress
 P – as in purity
U – as in ugliness
 S – as in sparkle
 A – as in amaranth.
Got it? Then continue writing,
please.

As the soul escaped from the girl's lips
and dissolved in the blue
the girl's mouth withered
like a broken flower.

The statuette still smiled,
a favourite of the girl while alive,
and then went smiling with her to the grave
to watch how presently
the angel of putrefaction
stepped close to the girl's body
and swiftly tore her skin
with purple nails.

For years the spectres hung about the spot
and with their voices terrified the living
who were nearby.
But all has long been silent there.

Only behind the holly bush
do pilgrims sometimes rest
and to their lips they raise the reed-pipes
they carry in their cloaks.

Where did I hear that song
of the girl's flimsy tunic?
She resisted so little
she was easily overcome.
Once it slid down the shoulder's curve
the palm was scarcely halted by the breast
when it found itself cupped in it
like a lamb that had strayed
        into a wolf-trap.

All that was left were some handfuls of dust,
no more.
He rose in the dark and again sat down
in the vast space of the tomb.
And through a crack between the slabs
like the barking of dogs
now and then burst
the fragrance of violets.

PLACE OF PILGRIMAGE

After a long journey we awoke
in the cathedral's cloisters, where men slept
on the bare floor.
There were no buses in those days,
only trams and the train,
and on a pilgrimage one went on foot.

We were awakened by the bells. They boomed
from square-set towers.
Under their clangour trembled not only the church
but the dew on the stalks
as though somewhere quite close above our heads
some elephants were trampling on the clouds
in a morning dance.

A few yards from us the women were dressing.
Thus did I catch a glimpse
for only a second or two
of the nakedness of female bodies
as hands raised skirts above heads.

But at that moment someone clamped
his hand upon my mouth
so that I could not even let out my breath
And I groped for the wall.

A moment later all were kneeling
before the golden reliquary
hailing each other with their songs.
I sang with them.
But I was hailing something different,
yes and a thousand times,
gripped by first knowledge.

The singing quickly bore my head away
out of the church.

In the Bible the Evangelist Luke
writes in his Gospel,
Chapter One Verse Twenty-six
and following:

And the winged messenger flew in by the window
into the virgin's chamber,
as softly as the barn-owl flies by night,
and hovered in the air before the maiden
a foot above the ground,
ceaselessly beating his wings.
He spoke in Hebrew about David's throne.

She only dropped her eyes in surprise
and whispered: Amen
and her nut-brown hair
fell from her forehead on her prie-dieu.

Now I know how at that fateful moment
those women act
to whom the angel has announced nothing.

They first shriek with delight,
then they sob
and mercilessly dig their nails
into man's flesh.
And as they close their lap
and tauten their muscles
a heart in tumult hurls wild words
up to their lips.

I was beginning to get ready for life
and headed wherever
the world was thickest.
On fairground stalls I well recall the rattle
of rosaries
like rain on a tin roof,
and the girls, as they strolled among the stalls,
nervously clutching their scarves,
liberally cast their sparkling eyes
in all directions,
and their lips launched on the empty air
the delight of kisses to come.

Life is a hard and agonizing flight
of migratory birds
to regions where each man is alone.
And whence there's no return.
And all that you have left behind,
the pain, the sorrows, all your disappointments
seem easier to bear
than is this loneliness,
where there is no consolation
to bring a little comfort to
your tear-stained soul.

What use to me are those sweet sultanas?
Good thing that at the rifle booth I won
a bright-red paper rose!   .
I kept it a long time
and still it smelled of carbide.

THE CANAL GARDEN

Not till old age did I learn
to love silence.
Sometimes it is more exciting than music.
In the silence emerge tremulous signals
and at the crossroads of memory
I hear names
which time had tried to stifle.

At nightfall in the trees I often hear
even the hearts of birds.
And once in the churchyard
I caught the sound, deep down in a grave,
of a coffin splitting.

On a forgotten stone block in the garden,
hewn in a sea-shell's shape,
the children used to play till dusk.
I can remember it from childhood.
And I'd still see them there.

It probably was the last stone surviving
from an old garden.
Nothing else was left.
Only a fountain and a tree,
only a violated fountain
and a half-shrivelled tree
whose trunk was perforated
by a revolver bullet.

Night, that merciless matron of darkness,
hurriedly pours the red dawn from the sky
like the bloody water
in which Monsieur Marat was murdered
by a fair-haired beauty's dagger,
and now it begins to rip off people's
own shadows
as a tailor rips off the tacked sleeves
when fitting a jacket.

Everything on earth has happened before,
nothing is new,
but woe to the lovers
who fail to discover a fresh blossom
in every future kiss.

The light still lies on the flower beds
and on the gentle path.
Among the flowers taking a walk
is Count Joseph Emanuel Canal de Malabaile
and with the hem of his exalted cloak
he bends the flower heads
which straighten up again at once.

       No admission for Jews!
       Well, really!

Each of us walks towards his own abyss.
There are two:
the deep sky overhead and the grave.
The grave is deeper.

By the pool's edge stands the statue of a goddess
hewn from white stone.
The damp sleek curves of her quivering body
are like whipped cream.

Where have your ancient dazzling skies gone
where you would tie your flaxen hair
in a honey-hued knot?
With slender arm you cover your breasts
and bend gently forward
as if about to step into the water
which is locked up by pale-pink water lilies
just unfolding.

Your lap, mirrored in the surface,
resembles Orpheus's divine instrument
which the Thracian women wrested from his hands
and flung into the Hebrus.

Upon the lintels of the doors they wrote
the year one thousand eight hundred and twenty-nine
with hallowed chalk.
In the stalls of the *Stavovské* Theatre
stood a poet
nervously waiting
for one of the boxes to open
and for the countess to enter.
Deep inside him at that moment screamed
enamoured folly.

He lived in Michalská Street
at the Red Cockerel,
and since he had no furniture
he wrote his poems lying on the floor,
dipping his pen in an inkstand
pinned to the floorboards.

Be quiet, clumps of roses,
don't whisper her name to me.
Reeds on the lake, be still
and do not rustle,
let me not hear the silk of her skirts
as she leaves for the waiting coach.

Never, never will she stroke
the thin beard on my chin,
never shall I sink my lips
into her body.
I wish I had never seen her,
then she would not have
chopped off my head each time
with the sword of her beauty.

The following day again he stood patiently
by the column in the theatre
fixedly staring at the empty box.
As she came in
and sat down in the velvet armchair
she briefly shut her bewitching eyes
with their long lashes
as a carnivorous plant closes its sticky blooms
from which there's no escape.

Oh shade your eyes, my love,
or I'll go mad.
He was young,
he went mad and died.

Night, eternal ant-heap of the stars,
and what else?
In the welcome shadow of the arbour
the lovers were kissing.

Lips kissed a hundred times
whispering ardent words to
lips kissed a hundred times,
lighting blood's path
pounding to passion's farthest regions.

A pair of daggers,
tongues mutually stabbed
desire-stirred mouths.

The evening star that night was Venus.

Let us return to the noble count.
He was fond of music
and instructed his musicians
to play their wind instruments
concealed in the garden's shrubberies.

The musicians breathed into their instruments
the heavy scent of flowers
and under the touch of their fingers
it changed into love songs
for dancing.

Here they are! If you feel like dancing
dance!

If the coral point
of one of the two rounded hills
of graceful obstinacy
wrote on my coat, as we were dancing,
a few letters from the Morse alphabet
this did not necessarily mean anything.
That happens.
It may even happen by chance.

But I would usually see it as
a call from another planet
orbiting round my forehead.
Someone perhaps will shrug:
What of it?
But I have given all my life
to just this call.

After the dance the weary lady would
sit down on the silky lawn,
spreading the muslin of her ample skirts
around herself
like spreading circles on the water.

I heard her carefree laughter
but I came too late.

As one grows old
one always comes too late,
and in the end one even envies the lawn
two dimples
made by a girl's knees.

I was lucky. Hand in hand
the exhilarated couples danced
on the trampled grass around the trees.
Only once in my life
did I meet that girl.

With a smile she invited me to her side,
the way people invite each other
when they sometimes feel
that a word would be too bold.
Presently she slowed her pace
to let me catch up with her.

Wherever you wish me to follow
I'll gladly go.
Even to the rock where sulphur flowers bloom
close to the crater's rim.

That far she didn't want to go with me.
A shiver ran over her
as if death had touched her.

At least give me your hand – goodbye.
She hesitated briefly
but, for goodbye,
she dug her lips into my mouth
like tiger's claws.

I look at your forehead
as a pilot at his cockpit panel
when he has flown into a storm.
I met you so late
and so unexpectedly.

I know you were hidden
in the deep drift of hair.
It glowed in the dark
but I sought you in vain.

On my empty palm
there was gold dust.

Then you escaped through the fence of your lashes
into your laughter.
And June, in festive garb,
pushed jasmine into our windows.

But in the end you vanish
into the snow of your silence.
How could I even catch a glimpse of you
that far away?
It was cold and dusk began to fall.

You may tear up my poems
and cast the shreds to the wind.
Crumple my letters
and burn them on the fire.

But what will you do with my face
cast in misted metal
no bigger than a hand?
You always had it before your eyes!
Do with it what your disappointment
leads you to do.

But one more time, one last time,
you will hold my head
between your hands.

The count is dead, the countess is dead,
the poet is dead.
The musicians are dead.
All my loves are dead,
and I myself am getting ready
to go.
At least that is how it sometimes seems to me
when I gaze
into your distant eyes
and in the distance vainly seek
the very last stone from the garden
which too is dead.

THE PLAGUE COLUMN

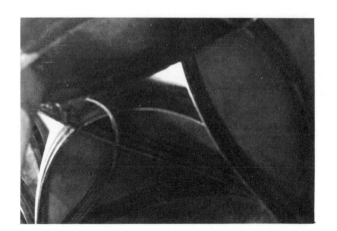

To the four corners of the earth they turn:
the four demobilized knights of the heavenly host.
And the four corners of the earth
are barred
behind four heavy locks.

Down the sunny path the ancient shadow
of the Column staggers
from the hour of Bondage
to the hour of Dance.
From the hour of Love
to the hour of the Dragon's Claw.
From the hour of Smiles
to the hour of Wrath.

From the hour of Hope
to the hour of Never
whence it is just a short step
to the hour of Despair
to Death's tourniquet.

Our lives run
like fingers over sandpaper,
days, weeks, years, centuries.
And there were times when we spent
long years in tears.

I still walk round the Column
where so often I waited,
listening to the water gurgling
from apocalyptic mouths,
always astonished
at the water's flirtatiousness
as it splintered on the basin's surface
until the Column's shadow fell across your face.

That was the hour of the Rose.

You there, young lad, do me a favour: climb
up on the fountain and read out to me
the words the four Evangelists are writing
on their stone pages.

The Evangelist Matthew is first.
> And which of us from pure joy
> can add to his life's span
> one cubit?

And what does Mark, the second, write?
> Is a candle brought
> to be put under a bushel
> and not to be set on a candlestick?

And the Evangelist Luke?
> The light of the body is the eye.
> But where many bodies are
> thither will many eagles be gathered
> together.

And lastly John, the favourite of the Lord,
what does he write?
He has his book shut on his lap.
Then open it, boy. If needs be
with your teeth.

I was christened on the edge of Olšany
in the plague chapel of Saint Roch.

When bubonic plague was raging in Prague
they laid the dead around the chapel.
Body upon body in layers.
Their bones, over the years, grew into
rough-stacked pyres
which blazed
in the quicklime whirlwind of clay.

For a long time I would visit
these mournful places
but I did not forsake the sweetness of life.

I felt happy in the warmth of human breath
and when I roamed among people
I tried to catch the perfume of women's hair.

On the steps of the Olšany taverns
I used to crouch at night to hear
the coffin-bearers and grave-diggers
singing their rowdy songs.

But that was long ago,
the taverns have fallen silent,
the grave-diggers in the end
buried each other.

When spring came within reach
with feather and lute
I'd walk around the lawn with the Japanese cherries
on the south side of the chapel
and, bewitched by their spring splendour,
I thought about girls
silently undressing at night.
I did not know their names
but one of them,
when sleep would not come,
tapped softly on my window.

And who was it that wrote
those poems on my pillow?

Sometimes I would stand by the wooden belfry
The bell was tolled
whenever they lifted up a corpse in the chapel.
It too is silent now.

I gazed on the classicist statuary
in the Little City cemetery.
The statues were still grieving over their dead
from whom they had had to part.
Leaving, they walked slowly
with the smile of their ancient beauty.

And there were among them not only women
but also soldiers with helmets, and armed
unless I'm mistaken.

I haven't been there for a long time.

Don't let them gull you
that the plague's at an end:
I've seen too many coffins hauled
through this dark gateway
which isn't the only one.

The plague still rages and it seems the doctors
are giving different names to the disease
to avoid a panic
Yet it is still the same old death
and nothing else,
and it is so contagious
no one alive can escape it.

Whenever I have looked out of my window
emaciated horses have been drawing that ill-boding cart
with a shrivelled coffin.
Those bells aren't tolled so often now,
crosses no longer painted on front doors,
juniper twigs no longer burnt for fumigation.

In the Julian Fields
we'd sometimes lie at nightfall,
when Brno was sinking into darkness,
and on the backwater of the Svitava
the frogs began their plaint.

Once a young gipsy sat down beside us.
Her blouse was half unbuttoned
and she read our hands.
To Halas she said:
                    You won't live to be fifty.
To Arthur Černík:
                    You'll live until just after that.
I didn't want her to tell my fortune,
I was afraid.

She seized my hand
and angrily exclaimed:
                    You'll live a long time!
It sounded like a threat.

The many rondels and the songs I wrote!
There was a war all over the world
and all over the world
was grief.
And yet I whispered into bejewelled ears
verses of love.
It makes me feel ashamed.
But no, not really.

A wreath of sonnets I laid upon
the curves of your lap as you fell asleep.
It was more beautiful than the laurel wreaths
of speedway winners.

But suddenly we met
at the steps of the fountain,
we each went somewhere else, at another time
and by another path.

For a long time I felt
I was meeting your feet,
sometimes I even heard your laughter
but it wasn't you.
And finally I even saw your eyes.
But only once.

My skin thrice dabbed with a swab
soaked in iodine
was golden brown.
The colour of the skin of dancing girls
in Indian temples.
I stared fixedly at the ceiling
to see them better
and the flower-decked procession
moved round the temple.

One of them, the one in the middle
with the blackest eyes,
smiled at me.
God,
what foolishness is racing through my head
as I lie on the operating table
with drugs in my blood.

And now they've lit the lamp above me,
the surgeon brings his scalpel down
and firmly makes a long incision.
Because I came round quickly
I firmly closed my eyes again.
Even so I caught a glimpse
of female eyes above a sterile mask
just long enough for me to smile.
Hallo, beautiful eyes.

By now they had ligatures round my blood-vessels
and hooks opening up my wounds
to let the surgeon separate
the paravertebral muscles
and expose the spines and arches.
I uttered a soft moan.

I was lying on my side,
my hands tied at the wrists
but with my palms free:
these a nurse was holding in her lap
up by my head.
I firmly gripped her thigh
and convulsively pressed it to me
as a diver clutches a slim amphora
streaking up to the surface.

Just then the pentothal began to flow
into my veins
and all went black before me.
There was a darkness as at the end of the world
and I remember no more.

Dear nurse, you had a few bruises.
I'm very sorry.
But in my mind I say:
                              A pity
I couldn't bring this alluring booty
up with me from the darkness
into the light and
before my eyes.

The worst is over now,
I tell myself: I'm old.
The worst is yet to come:
I'm still alive.
If you really must know:
I have been happy.
Sometimes a whole day, sometimes whole hours,
sometimes just a few minutes.

All my life I have been faithful to love.
And if a woman's hands are more than wings
what then are her legs?
How I enjoyed testing their strength.
That soft strength in their grip.
Let then those knees crush my head!

If I closed my eyes in this embrace
I would not be so drunk
and there wouldn't be that feverish drumming
in my temples.
But why should I close them?

With open eyes
I walked through this country.
It's beautiful – but you know.
It has meant more to me perhaps than all my loves
and her embrace has lasted all my life.
When I was hungry
I fed almost daily
on the words of her songs.

Those who have left,
who have hastily fled to distant lands
must be aware of it:
the world is terrible.
They do not love and are not loved.
We at least love.

So let her knees then crush
my head!

Here is an accurate catalogue of guided missiles.

Surface-to-air
Surface-to-surface
Surface-to-sea
Air-to-air
Air-to-surface
Air-to-sea
Sea-to-air
Sea-to-sea
Sea-to-surface

Be quiet, city, I can't hear the weir.
And people go about, quite unsuspecting
that above their heads fly
fiery kisses
delivered by hand from window to window.

Mouth-to-eye
Mouth-to-face
Mouth-to-mouth
And so on

Until a hand at night pulls down a blind
and hides the target.

On the narrow horizon of home
between sewing box
and slippers with swansdown pompoms
her belly's hot moon
is quickly waxing.

Already she counts the days of the lark
though the sparrows are still pecking poppyseed
behind the frost-etched flowers.

In the wild-thyme nest
someone's already winding up the spring
of the tiny heart
so it should go accurately
all life long.

What's all this talk of grey hair
and wisdom?
When the bush of life burns down
experience is worthless.
Indeed it always has been.

After the hailstorm of graves
the Column was thrust up high
and four old poets
leaned on it with their backs
to write on the books' pages
their bestsellers.

The basin now is empty,
littered with cigarette stubs
and the sun only hesitantly uncovers
the grief of the stones pushed aside.
A place perhaps for begging.

But to cast my life away just like that
for nothing at all – that
I won't do.

MERRY-GO-ROUND WITH WHITE SWAN

Where the pavement had turned
into tufts of grass
and the electric wires into swallows' wings
two carbide lamps
were lit every evening in spring
and swiftly engulfed by the night,
and the ancient merry-go-round started turning.

The pool of light was quietly avoided
by the late couples
who hugged each other under the thick shrub of darkness
dotted with stars.

For the most beautiful of all gods
is Love.
It always has been thus, and everywhere,
not only in distant turquoise Greece
but even in our lousy Žižkov quarter
where the city either began
or ended. Whichever you like.
And where the singing in the taverns
went on till dawn.

On the edge among the horses' hooves
grandly and elegantly an aristocratic swan
sailed past,
as if snatched straight from a poem by Mallarmé.
And spread its wings.

That afternoon there was a brief shower
that made even the trampled grass smell sweet,
and the evening, full of vernal yearnings,
slowly melted into night.

The hurdy-gurdy had just begun
to chop up a new tune
when a girl with a silver bracelet
stepped into the swan's wings.

I noticed her wrist
because she embraced the swan's neck
and her eyes
looked past my enflamed glances.

In the end she looked at me
and smiled a little,
and next time round she waved to me,
the third time round blew me a kiss.
That was all.

I waited for her next appearance,
ready to jump on board and join her,
but the wings were empty.

Love sometimes is like the flower
of the wild poppy:
you can't carry it home.
But the two lamps were hissing loud
like a pair of snakes
snake confronting snake,
and I was vainly chasing after her feet
into the vast darkness.

There was a time when they fired a cannon on the walls
to announce midday,
and for a breath-long second the hustle stopped.
Some women are Morning, some are Noontide
and some are Evening.

Hesitant fingers gently roaming
over the skin of coyness,
until modesty and fear begin to flee from the places
we so love,
and a wave of nakedness, wave after wave,
floods our mouths and eyes and cheeks
and again returns to our lips
as to the shore.

Thus our blood began to flow
into their veins
and thence to the heart and from the heart
back into our arteries.

Neither greed for power nor thirst for glory
are as dizzy
as the passions of love.
Even if perhaps
I wasn't one of those
to be granted overmuch
I gratefully kissed its feet.

When it appears to me that women today
are maybe more beautiful
than they were in my youth
this is only delusion and surmise.
Nothing but bitter nostalgia. And regrets.

Not long ago I was looking at
the yellowed photographs of Mucha's models
in his Paris studio.
The startling charm of these long bygone women
took my breath away.

There were two wars, disease and famine
and a cluster of suffering.
Life was not good on earth in those days.
But it was truly our life
no matter how it was.

I used to yearn for distant cities
in colourful strange countries
even on the edge of the desert.
Now they are rapidly receding
like the stars in the age-old darkness.
There is a chill in the cathedrals
and women's smiles
have become rare and strange and faraway
like blooms in the jungle.

Only the yearning has remained: not to be so lonely,
and my curiosity.
And daily I am catechized by these.
I am thankful our women do not wear
a veil down to their ankles.
But inexorable time now presses me
and forcibly leads me elsewhere.

Good-bye. In all my life I never committed
any betrayal.
That I am aware of
and you may believe me.

But the most beautiful of all gods
is Love.

EPILOGUES

A CHAPLET OF SAGE
For František Hrubín

Noon was approaching and the quiet
was cut by the buzzing of the flies
as though with a diamond.
We were lying in the grass by the Sazava,
drinking Chablis
chilled in a forest spring.

Once at Konopiště Castle
I was allowed to view
an ancient dagger from a display case.
Only in the wound did a secret spring
release a triple blade.
Poems are sometimes like that.
Not many of them perhaps,
but it is difficult to extract them from the wound.

A poet often is like a lover.
He easily forgets
his once-time whispered promise of gentleness
and the most fragile gracefulness
he treats with brutal gesture.

He has the right to rape
Under the banner of beauty
or that of pain.
Or under the banner of both.
Indeed it is his mission.

Events themselves hand him
a ready pen
that with its tip he may indelibly tattoo
his message.

Not on the skin of the breast
but straight into the muscle
which throbs with blood.
But rose and heart are not just love,
nor a ship a voyage or adventure,
nor a knife murder,
nor an anchor fidelity unto death.

These foolish symbols lie.
Life has long outgrown them.
Reality is totally different
and a lot worse still.

And so the poet drunk with life
should spew out all bitterness,
anger and despair,
rather than let his song become a tinkling bell
on a sheep's neck.

When we had drunk our fill
and rose from the flattened grass
a bunch of naked children on the bank
hopped into the river below us.
And one of the young girls,
the one who on her straw-blond hair
wore a chaplet of wet sage,
climbed up on a large rock
to stretch out on the sun-warmed stone.

We had a slight shock:
                    Good Lord,
she's no longer a child!

THE MODEL

I wish they'd wrap that rug around me
and carry me back to the studio,
to the warm stove.
And pour hot punch down my throat.

I'm standing here naked in the shade
to allow Maestro Hynais
to get the exact
shade of a body blue with cold
for his portrayal of Winter.

He had, I'm told, sought for a long time
a redhead like me,
with slate-coloured icy eyes.
If I had raven hair
and red eyes like a mouse

I wouldn't be standing here.
And he wouldn't have hung these transparent drapes on me
these transparent drapes on me.
So slowly, so deliberately.
Once, to catch the outline of my breasts –
yes, I've got good ones –
the next time so my thighs should show
with the gooseflesh.
Each time the professor would step back a little,
he'd change the folds of the material
and I'd go on freezing.

Get on with it, you old fool!
You're wearing winter boots and a fur coat
and I'm here naked
in a thin, transparent rag.

I could bear the cold on my back
but the wind's blowing right at me
and here in front I have two lumps of ice;
it still feels as if someone were pushing pins
into my nipples.

What do you really know about the female body?
Women are delicate about their bellies
and when we catch a chill down there
it's a disaster for quite a while.

To hell with your picture,
to hell with the anteroom of the Royal Box.
Am I to freeze to death for Art?
To hell with your National Theatre!
You'll earn your fame
and I pneumonia.
A favourite cause of death
and quite frequent, in case you didn't know.

Don't stand there thinking but paint,
or I'll knock that palette from your hand
and trample it in the snow.
I'm not purple enough, you say?
And though my teeth are rattling
like skeletons in a Punch and Judy show –
that's not enough?

I wished you'd stayed in your Paris!
The last street girl
wouldn't have posed for you like this.
And there's a place for every kind of slut,
ready for anything.

I wish they'd come with that rug,
that coarse but warming rug,
I wish they'd come.

NOCTURNAL DARKNESS

Only now, at the late hour of my life,
when I can no longer go anywhere,
have I read that here in Bohemia
they used to call the slender mullein
a sun-rod.

I've still a little time
to write these few verses
but not too much when I remember
the dark hours of the night.

First, those delicious ones
with you!
The moon did not rise, the stars did not shine,
the lamps between the trees were far away
and you moreover closed your eyes.

On our way home the only light
was your forehead
Then those when we strayed about
the blacked-out city.
All windows were obscured
and behind many of them people were crying
to break your heart.

Those heaps of flowers on the Jewish furnaces
and behind the Red Hall,
and until recently here at Břevnov
in the abandoned quarry!

As when the Roman soldiery
thrust their lances into the ground
and lay down beside them
either to throw dice a little longer
or to lie down to sleep.

THE STRIKING OF THE TOWER CLOCK
For Cyril Bouda

That evening, when night was already at the door
and the pigeon droppings on the cornices of the towers
resembled the moon's light,
I was listening to a Vivaldi air
in the Maltese Garden.

A girl was playing it on a silver flute.
But what can a slender instrument
in a girl's fingers conceal?
Hardly anything!
At times I forgot to listen.

Below the bridge murmured the distant wier:
not even water will put up with fetters
and revolts in the spillway.

Almost imperceptibly she was beating time
with the point of her slipper
with her lips she coaxed the ancient air
into the ancient garden.
From far away. From a city in the South,
where among the veins of the lagoons
the city sits on the wrist of the sea.

The air made every fibre in her vibrate.
And although the amorous notes
were full of seduction,
the girl's charm at that moment was so defenceless
that even in my thoughts I did not have the boldness
or would encourage the idea
of touching her blush with as much as
the tip of a finger.

In that smiling play of darkness and flute,
of the striking of the hours from the tower
and of obliquely shooting stars,
when it was possible to hurry somewhere upstairs,
up a vertiginous flight
without holding on to the bannisters,
I convulsively clutched the metal
of my French cane.

When the applause died away
it seemed that, from the dusk of the nearby park,
the whispers could be heard
and the hesitant footfall of lovers.

But their ardent kisses,
as you probably know,
already are the first tears of love.
And all great love affairs on earth
end tragically.

THE BIRD'S VOICES IN THE TREE TOPS

Only a small wrought-iron gate that's always open
bars entry to the Pleasure Garden
and the white loggia
at the end of the avenue of ancient limes.
I used to go there and to listen for
the long-dead footfall of the poet Macha
on the damp flagstones
amidst the jubilant amorous songs
above and all around.

I know, birds foul a lot of things,
even the pure eyes of forget-me-nots,
and some of them even lurk by the hives
and murder bees,
adroitly removing their stings.
But this is their kingdom.

And when on our window-sill in March
the first blackbird sings out
it is like the voice of the signal bell
on a rural platform,
with the train already pulling out of the next station.

Above the Pleasure Garden is Zebín Hill.
On its summit
the compass needle is deflected
and flickers like my heart
when on the loggia steps I see
your legs.

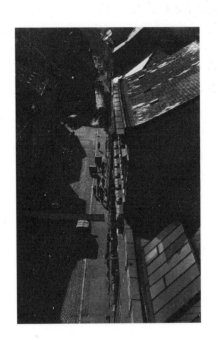

IN AN EMPTY ROOM

Even the raven belongs to the song bird family
and that gives me courage
when sadness like a stifling smog
falls on my life.
What price sweet verses
when a man is old.
Even the whiteness of the snow revolts him.

But for you, nonetheless, I'd like to bring along
a little white dove.
If you held it in your hands
it would softly peck your finger.
I see it often on the roof across the road
and could invite it over.
It has come from afar,
from King Solomon's love songs.
Gently press it to your breast,
that's where it belongs.
But if it flies up with the others
it is a momentary flash of glitter
like a mirror caught in the sun.

You can stay silent if you don't feel like talking,
only please smile,
and when you give me
a kiss not only on my cheek
but also on my lips,
I want to feel your hot breath.
How greedy I am.

I remember the days when it was much darker
in the cinemas than today.
The films were darker and moreover
the screen always looked as if it were raining.
Only above the doors glowed dim red bulbs
in case of panic.

In those days young people kissed
not only hidden in dark boxes
but also in the back row of the stalls.
In thirst I drank saliva from the mouths of girls.
It was intoxicating like chewed betel juice
but that is a deep red
and burns on the tongue.

THE SONG OF THE NIGHTINGALE

I am a hunter of sounds and a collector
of tape recordings.
I listen to huntsmen sounding the mort on the radio
on very short waves.
Let me show you my collection.

The nightingale's song. It's fairly well known
but this nightingale
is a kinsman of those to whom Neruda listened
when he turned the heads of Prague's young beauties.
Added to the recording is the amplified sound
of a bursting bud
as the rose petals begin to unfold.

And here are a few gloomy recordings.
A person's death-rattle.
The recording is absolutely authentic.
The creaking of the hearse and the rhythm
of the horses' hooves on the paving stones.
Then the solemn fanfares from the National Theatre
at Josef Hora's funeral.

All these I acquired by swapping.
But the tape
"Frozen earth on my mother's coffin"
is my own recording.

Then follow Chevalier and Mistinguette,
the charming Josephine Baker
with a cluster of ostrich feathers.
Among the younger ones the graceful Greco and Mathieu
with their new discs.

And finally you shall hear the passionate whispering
of two unknown lovers.
No, the words are difficult to make out,
you only hear the sighs.
And then the sudden silence
ended by a sigh –
the moment
when tired lips are glued
to tired lips.

It is a restful moment
not a kiss.

Yes, you may be right:
the moment after love-making
resembles death.

THE SMOKE OF MARIJUANA

To bow at the footlights
and sink into a curtsy,
as the French do on the stage –
no, that's not for me.
But no sooner had I written
a few happy lines about love
than my eyes would seek the eyes of women,
my hands their hands
and my lips their startled lips.

God knows, in this country
women like poetry.
Maybe that's why the poet's sighs
don't make them press their hands so frantically
upon their breasts.

When I was still young
and learned to woo women,
oh, my conceit
was more pretentious
than a peacock's fan,
which is blue and pink and golden
like Renoir's palette.

Deceiving myself thus
I happily came to the end,
to despair,
which some call wisdom.
I can't think why.

But at that moment someone at my back
whispered into my ear:
Like marijuana smoke
are poets' verses.
And if that perfumed smoke
opens the door to some exotic country,
whence delicious moments of happiness, smiling,
run up to meet us,
holding hands
with happy moments of delight –
why shouldn't poetry achieve it too?

One single song is enough
to make people catch their breath
and make girls, when they hear it,
burst into tears.

How I should like to possess that skill!
Especially now,
when I am old and shuffle about
and my words grate in my teeth.

But if I listened to the silence
and forced my pen –
what do you think you'd hear?

At best the song
which Jan Jakub Ryba sang
with his throat cut,
as the razor dropped from his hand
and he stood leaning against that pine tree
alone, all alone,
in the woods near Rožmitál.

AND NOW GOODBYE

To all those million verses in the world
I've added just a few.
They probably were no wiser than a cricket's chirrup.
I know. Forgive me.
I'm coming to the end.

They weren't even the first footmarks
in the lunar dust.
If at times they sparkled after all
it was not their light.
I loved this language.

And that which forces silent lips
to quiver
will make young lovers kiss
as they stroll through red-gilded fields
under a sunset
slower than in the tropics.

Poetry is with us from the start.
Like loving,
like hunger, like the plague, like war.
At times my verses were embarassingly
foolish.

But I make no excuse.
I believe that seeking beautiful words
is better
than killing and murdering.